PUSSY POWER

WOMEN'S EMPOWERMENT THROUGH POEMS TO PONDER AND PICTURES TO COLOR

LYNNE SULLIVAN, MFT
ILLUSTRATED BY JORIE MARTIN

PUSSY SISTERS PRESS

LOS ANGELES

Pussy Power: Women's Empowerment Through Poems to Ponder and Pictures to Color

Author: Lynne Sullivan
Illustrator: Jorie Martin
Book Designer: Marty Safir, Double M Graphics

PUSSY SISTERS PRESS
LOS ANGELES, CALIFORNIA
www.pussysisters.com

For inquiries contact info@pussysisters.com

ISBN-13: 978-0-578-76380-4

DEDICATED TO PUSSIES EVERYWHERE
AND TO THOSE WHO RESPECT THEM

PREFACE

This book is about the empowerment of women. It is the result of not weeks or even months of work, but of years—hundreds of years—of the struggles of women to be recognized as equals.

The idea that "All men are created equal" is no longer suitable and never was. Sure, the use of the word "men" is supposed to be inclusive of all beings regardless of sex, but the word itself shows a bias that has pervaded society since there have been societies. Perhaps we should look forward to the day that "All human beings are created equal," keeping in mind that equality does not mean "sameness." Women are driven from within by unique, creative forces that are the essence of femininity, and need not be sacrificed in a quest to be "equal," but to be honored as equally powerful.

We wrote this book with the hopes that it will inspire others—regardless of gender—to recognize that we are at a new crossroads that must be noticed, acknowledged, and discussed. The political climate of today is producing red flags by the dozens that point to the inequities that still exist for women in our society. The unfortunate side effect of letting these biases persist is that they continue to chip away at the very essence of what women need and deserve—to be respected, having equal rights so that they have unlimited potential to seek, find, and realize their dreams.

We also created this book to delight. The whimsical and fanciful nature of many of these pages will lend balance to the seriousness of the subject matter. The book is also designed to be interactive, allowing the reader to participate through the use of their own creativity, colored pencils, and pens. And of course, it is also meant to instill deeper thought—and ultimately, action—that will produce a more productive and meaningful society.

The use of the words Pussy Power has allowed women to own the words that others have used in a negative way. The use of Pussy Hats has provided symbolism to seeing these words in a positive way. And whether intended or not, these words can put a smile on the face of millions of women (and already-enlightened men) who can appreciate a book like this in a serious yet enjoyable way.

–The Pussy Sisters

TABLE OF CONTENTS

Rosa Parks inspired me to find a way to get in the way, to get in trouble... good trouble, necessary trouble.

– JOHN LEWIS

PUSSY POWER

Pussy Hat March

Women marching
proudly
hearts open
pumping wildly
feet stomping
to protest
for
their rights
their Children's rights
the rights of all
women
for generations

Woman dancing
singing
yelling
marching
across the globe

In sisterhood
their unity
spreading light
Their power within
shining and growing
in pride
as they
embrace
their human rights

By Invitation Only

Finger painting
her
self-worth
she swirled her fingers
in the thick paint
reveling in it's velvety
texture
"Sparkle next," she mused
as
she added stones
bits of gold
and rhinestones

We are women, she thought
so similar
yet so very different

We are irreplaceable...
Our laugh, our gait
our thoughts, our dreams
are cherished
by
those who love us

Each inch of our skin
an intimate playground
for
frolic, fun
and reverence
by invitation only

My Gift

I give you
respect,
that you may
respect yourself

I admire
the qualities
that are
intrinsically you

I instill
within you
a sense of worth
by
appreciating your
accomplishments

I provide
a soft
place to land
creating a space
for
self-discovery

I share
the stories
of my life
painful, embarrassing, proud
All taught me
Lessons
They are
my gift to you

Growing ever wise
and capable
with outstretched arms
I release you
to embrace
the world
with a sense of purpose
and dignity

Earth Mother

Earth Mother
so soft
empathetic
and
enticing

Her large
desert eyes
invite one
to open their heart

This is her gift

Earth Mother
whose roots
grow wide
and deep
as she weathers
the turmoil presented to her
with a knowing
gaze

She has soothed
many tears,
an anchor
for those she
embraces
The wrinkles
surrounding her eyes
the only
outward sign

Earth Mother
grounded by her
love for others
she absorbs and heals
their pain
with an
outstretched hand
a fully bodied hug
and
a mug of hot deliciousness

Little Red Riding Hood

She loved nature
and hence the woods
She loved her Grandma
and wanted to bring
her treats

Once inside
Grandma's home
she was observant—
some things were different
bigger eyes
large glistening teeth
She focused
inside herself
where her intuition lives
Her stomach felt icky
Her hair stood up
She felt creepy
DANGER

Her body
flew into action
fought off the wolf
and then
blogged about it
after she returned
to the safety
of her home

Thank goodness
for
self-defense classes!

I Celebrate

I am fire and water
I am stardust and earth
My power emanates from
my boundaries and principles
my intuition and heart
my persistence and compassion

My power and strength
come from deep within
my knowing
who I am
why I am here
and
the purpose
for
my existence

Annie Oakley

She grew up
knowing
what she loved
Fierce and forbidden
she pursued them
despite
possible consequences

She was electrified
by the smell
of the
gunpowder
The sound of
the bullet hitting its inanimate target
captivated her

She especially loved
showing others her skills
Practicing relentlessly
Annie
outshot most men

Word traveled far
Invited to
perform
she shared her talent
with
the world

While
entertaining others
she embarked on
a career of taboo
becoming
the first woman sharpshooter

Mona Lisa

Some say Mona Lisa was mysterious
Some say she was a visionary
determined to do as she wished

Despite threats
of
bringing ruin
to her reputation
she did as she pleased
Sitting for hours
as rumors swirled
Little did she know
her likeness
would be hidden
stolen
vandalized
and
ultimately restored

Her image becoming
symbolic
an infamous treasure
and
her smile
the ultimate
mystery

"The Future Belongs to Those Who Believe in the Beauty of Their Dreams"

E. ROOSEVELT

ELEANOR ROOSEVELT
First Lady *of the* World

Perspective

Symbolic
of freedom...
hat held gently
by
Mother Natures' hand
rising

A glimpse below
creates elation
encouragaing
perspective to widen
as priorities
shift

Walls seem
to dissolve as
focus intensifies
and narrows
onto
nearby trees and flowers

The sound of birds
singing their bedtime tunes
Become ALL
as
worldly noise fades

Challenges shrink
even gridlock at dusk
mesmerizes the senses
as freeways
transform
into a red and white
gilded bracelet
glittering
with
birdsongs as backdrop

Statue of Liberty

Battered by wind
having weathered waves
and years
of storms
Still she stands
Tall

With an outstretched arm
while
holding the torch
she alone illuminates
the Path

Her presence
a welcoming symbol
of freedom
and
opportunities

"The American Dream"
fills the hearts
of Immigrants
with hope

Queen of Hearts

She can win one over
with a smile
Her magnetism
is contagious
drawing
from Love
of a
Divine nature

She moves others
by unlocking
their hearts
She inspires
through her compassion
through her empathy
through her powerful example

She takes time
savoring
the simple pleasures
life has to offer
as
she caresses
every moment
releasing it
only after fully
devouring
and
processing
each morsel
like a Queen
The Queen
of Hearts

Susan B Anthony

A Goddess
of
self-reliance
a courageous visionary
traveling the US
sharing her ideas
ideas which would
spark a relentless flame
a flame
which she would
never see
come to fruition

Her vision
kept her
focused and strong
She gained her strength
through
persistence
and
civil disobedience

Standing with her
Sisters
beside her
sowing seeds of equality
for ALL women

She Persisted

Women
along with children
were to be seen
and
not heard

Without a voice
devoid of rights
how can anyone feel seen
if they are not heard?

So
Women
have persisted in this quest

They use their voices
quietly at first
then loudly expressing
ideas, opinions, hopes
and dreams

Their voices speak truths
which undulate with a vitality
so great
as to propel their words
of passion
into
the crowds

Words
which lodge themselves
into the minds
of those who truly
hear them
They fly through the air
dancing on branches
and
whirling through meadows
out
into the world
to create change

Queen of Diamonds

She lives life
in a constant quest
for truth
and
ever deepening
awareness

Gathering energy
from
each challenge
she delights in conquering
impossible obstacles

She ignites motivation
driven by
intuition and creativity
coupled with
reason and experience

Her tenacity and wisdom
gained over the decades
are
her assets
she wears like a cloak
of Light
emanating from within

She gladly shares
her abundance
to
assist other Queens
along the way

Sister Power

When women bond
to work together
it's magic
Obstacles melt
as
ideas flourish, bouncing
off one another
and the walls
Cohesion forms

Energy growing
walls melt
Excitement coupled with shrill exchanges
emerge
as differing points of view
collide
Compromise and respect
lead to solutions

When women are in need,
are in pain,
are in danger,
it is her sisters
who flock to her

Her sisters come to her aid
with hugs
words of encouragement
hot meals
babysitting
cleaning
first aid
safety plans

Women create a cocoon
of compassion and love
surrounding their sisters
filling their needs
until they can heal
rise up
and once again
join the world

Madam Butterfly

The Butterfly,
a symbol of
Transformation
for women and those who
identify as such
It is
a larger symbol

Representative of hope
and acceptance
for women of all shades,
shapes, and backgrounds

Flitting from flower to flower,
sucking the nectar
from each experience
as she learns to navigate

Gliding past the thorns,
through majestic and mangled tree branches,
over rugged mountains,
as she persists

As she soars above previous limitations,
she is unfettered by rules of the past
ready to reconstruct her life
Safety plan in place,
she is fearless

Armored in self-defense
and self-respect
she strolls down the road
to mingle with others

A world without fear
of predation and abuse,
a world without societal restraints
or rules
on how high she can fly

This Butterfly has a dream

We Endure

I will take my wounds
and
love them
I will tuck them
into my pocket
warm, safe
snuggling as they melt
into the lining
of my soul
held, honored, healed
and
Transformed

They shall be woven into
the fabric of
my essence
Proud scars
reminders of
my deep well
my shiny tapestry
woven of resilience
and
strength
it shall
carry me forward

Queen of Spades

She leads others
by shining her light
She leads
by example
assisting others
in their pursuits
with her open heart

Her communications
provide warmth
blanketed in care
empowering others
by allowing
spontaneous
ideas to spring forth

Her generous nature
demonstrates strength
by
embracing each persons'
individuality with
absolute delight

The Cat's Meow

Furry creature
nestled in flowers
ready to
explore
and
receive love

The secret
to her
power
is
in knowing
her worth

Pussy Pride
brings
boundaries
endurance
marches
and
self-respect

A Purrrrfect
prescription
for the
cat's meow

Sappho

An exotic woman
from Greece
she
listened to the music
of
the Universe
dancing in her ears
and
spun the sounds
into
words

Sensitive to Life's
vibrations
rich poetry
poured from her well
with
fervor and longings

She loved fiercely
with a passion
so intense
it mesmerized others
much like her poetry

It was said
she loved freely
with abandon
both men and women
appreciating the differences
in their fragrances and physiques
preferring variety
as a lush bouquet
for the banquet
of
her life

*You may forget, but
Let me tell you this:
Someone, in some
future time,
Will think of us.*

SAPPHO – CIRCA 600 BCE

Women Who Work at Home

Women who work at home
create a perfect space
for
their particular family

Whether others
come first
or they model self-care
they scrub and dust
They prune, plant,
and wash

Women who work at home
create meals that nourish
and delight
They chop, boil, braise,
and bake

The aromas
permeate the home
drawing even the most
playful child
to the table

Women who work at home
create rituals
which ground us
in predictability
sustaining us
during life's painful moments

Favorite songs, books, bath time games
and bedtime rituals
all become folded
into the recipes
of
Lifes' Magic Moments
sustaining us
with feelings of comfort
and love
throughout our lives

Harriet Tubman

Born a slave
she witnessed the cruelty
first hand
her skull split open
"master" missing the intended target
a mere child, left for dead
~but~
she did not die
Instead she grew up,
grew strong,
growing ever more determined

Once free in the North
she drove her horse and buggy
through the darkness,
back into the dangerous South
despite threats
from hooded devils
with their fiery vigils
of terror
She drove her buggy
bringing her people
from the South
into the light of freedom

They called it, "The Freedom Train"
her horse,
her buggy,
her faith, courage,
and determination
running against
time
through the night

They called it "The Freedom Train"
but
She was the train
She was the hope
for a life
of dignity and respect

Amelia Earhart

Inquisitive
she saw possibilities
where most women
only saw obstacles
Her challenges
were conquered
with zest

She led the way
radiating positivity
while
mentoring others

When
pursuing science
Amelia
exuberantly
wrote of her adventures

She viewed adventures
as events
to be devoured
and savored

Her writing became
intoxicating to
women seeking
an extraordinary life

She carved new paths
engaging in one of her
many joys
soaring
She flew her plane
shattering invisible ceilings
by
tearing down limitations

She broke new ground
allowing women
to embrace their own visions

Queen of Clubs

The Queen of Clubs
in her quest for knowledge
her curiosity
so insatiable
she holds center court
in
all meetings
with open ears

Her words
so direct and sharp
she leads the way
creating clarity
and
truth
in all endeavors

Underneath
her direct authority
lives an intuitive
heart
filled with caring
and
wonder for ALL

We Grab Back

When you see us
you don't see
Who we are

Invisible is our inner life,
rich and complex

You see
large eyes,
pouty plump lips
You check out
our curves
and hips

You don't see
our ambitions,
our goals,
the multiple
roles which
shape us

You focus on
our dewy soft skin
the size of our
breasts

You think
because we talk softly
laugh or smile
that we are yours
to paw or kiss
or to corner

We are cordial,
not weak
we are civil,
not pushovers

So remember
not to grab
because
We grab back!

We Grab Back

Determined

A small woman
with a huge
spirit
determined to raise
her three kids...alone

She worked at
a tavern
in the Midwest
Mother of Pearl
pistol in hand
as she closed the bar
each night
barely making ends meet
She learned
to do without

Then came the war
and jobs
once only held
by men
opened doors

Determined to raise
her three kids...alone
she welded baby buggies
The buggies were heavy
The machines hard to handle
sweat poured over
her body as she
worked

When the war ended
women were released from
their positions so the men
could go back to work

A small woman
with a bigger spirit
still determined to raise
her three kids...alone
returned to the Tavern

WE CAN DO IT!

ROSIE THE RIVETER

Embrace Yourself

Bodies are the packages
we show to
the world
Some
are wrapped
in glittered
paper
others
plain newsprint
accessorized
with clothing
and sometimes
embellished

Our body
is our
vehicle
for life
our unique
DNA
makes
everyone an
original Jewel

Hold it gently
learn its
textures, folds, crevices
and
cherish them
Appreciate its form
by nourishing it well
providing it safe restful spaces
and
respect it

Our bodies
provide a
protective shell
and our own
unique embodiment
of
Self

Girly Girls

I can
paint my face
or my apartment
or my nails
I'm a girly girl

I can
change outfits
change diapers
or change the oil in my car
I'm a girly girl

I can date
be a mom
become a mechanic
have a partner or not
I'm a girly girl

I am a doctor, a lawyer, a chef
I clean houses, I pick fruit in the orchards
and
I'm a girly girl

I dance
I sing
I perform
if I choose
just for you
I'm a girly girl

I can do
and be
a myriad of
of things
I do them all well
I'm a girly girl

Do not define me
I am ever growing
ever evolving
I am a girly girl

Notorious

Steely blue eyes
cut to the
truth

Powerful words
dissolve boundaries
and
injustice

Slow and steady
measured and precise
patient yet unyielding

Decade after decade
she chipped away
at the
inequality
that diminishes
the creation of
opportunities for
a better world

THE VOTING BOOTH is the only place that a pauper equals a billionaire, and any woman equals a man.

– Gloria Steinem

APPENDIX

Susan B. Anthony 1820 - 1906
Susan was born in Adams, Massachusetts at a time when women had few rights. She spent most of her life fighting social injustices, and was a key figure in advancing women's rights to vote. She was also an abolitionist against slavery. With her friend, Elizabeth Stanton, she started feminist publications, and together they took part in many acts of civil disobedience.

Amelia Earhart 1897 - 1937
Amelia was born in Atchison, Kansas. She was a popular author who inspired women through her colorful books depicting her travel adventures. She was influential in broadening the scope of possibilities for women and was best known as the first female to fly solo across the Atlantic. Fascination with Amelia's life, career, and disappearance continues to this day.

Ruth Bader Ginsburg 1933 - 2020
Ruth was born in Brooklyn, New York. She was an Associate Justice of the Supreme Court of the United States, appointed by president Bill Clinton. Ginsburg spent much of her legal career as an advocate for the advancement of gender equality and women's rights, winning multiple victories arguing before the Supreme Court. Ginsburg has received fame in American popular culture for her fiery liberal dissents and refusal to step down. She has been dubbed the "Notorious R.B.G."

Mona Lisa painting 1503 - 1506
The Mona Lisa, or La Gioconda, is a portrait painting by Italian Renaissance artist Leonardo da Vinci. Throughout history, Mona Lisa's mysterious smile has inspired poets and others to speculate about her identity, her life, and her secrets.

Annie Oakley 1860 – 1926
Annie was born in Darke County, Ohio. She broke through barriers and sexual stereotypes for women when she became known as one of America's sharp shooters. Eventually she was asked to join Buffalo Bill's Wild West Show. Famous quote: *"I ain't afraid to love a man. I ain't afraid to shoot one, neither."*

Rosy, the Riveter 1942
Rosy, the Riveter is a cultural icon of World War II, representing the women who worked in factories and shipyards during the war, many of whom produced munitions and war supplies. They often replaced male workers who joined the military.

Rosie is a symbol of American feminism and women's economic power. Some say that Rosie forever opened the work force for women, but others dispute that point, noting that many women were let go after the war when their jobs were given to returning servicemen. But the "Rosies" and the generations who followed learned that working outside the home was a possibility for women. Women did not, however, reenter the job market in large numbers until the 1970's.

ELEANOR ROOSEVELT 1884 - 1962

Eleanor was an outspoken supporter of the African-American civil rights movement. She broke with precedent by inviting hundreds of African-American guests to the White House. She insisted that benefits be equally extended to all Americans regardless of race or gender. She encouraged her husband, President Franklin Roosevelt, to appoint more women to federal positions, fought for higher wages for women, and held numerous press conferences for female reporters only, at a time when women were barred from White House conferences.

SAPPHO c. 630 – 570 BC

Sappho was born in Lesbos, Greece. She became known for her lyric poetry, which was often set to music and performed live. Her poetry was passionate and sensual, while rumors swirled about her liaisons with both men and women. Hundreds of years later, in the 19th Century, Sappho became a symbol for Women's Rights and a lifestyle of autonomy in both sexuality and social behavior.

STATUE OF LIBERTY 1886

The Statue of Liberty stands near Ellis Island, in the New York Harbor, in New York. The copper statue, a gift from the people of France to the people of the United States, was designed by French Sculptor, Frederic Auguste Bartholdi, and was dedicated in October, 1886. She is an icon of freedom and a welcoming sight to immigrants arriving to the United States from abroad.

The Statue of Liberty's famous inscription is from a poem The New Colossus, written by Emma Lazarus in 1883:

"Give me your tired, your poor,
your huddled masses
yearning to breathe free,
The wretched refuse of your teeming shore
Send these, the homeless,
tempest-tossed to me.
I lift my lamp beside the golden door."

HARRIET TUBMAN 1822 - 1913

Harriet was born in Dorchester County, Maryland. Her parents were both slaves. Over the course of her life she would become a Civil War nurse, a suffragist, a Civil Rights activist, and an abolitionist. She was best known for her courage as she transported slaves from the South to safety and freedom in the North. This became known as the Underground Railroad. Harriet continued to help her people, creating a home for black aging seniors who were physically failing with no access to resources.

This passage from one her speeches is eerily relevant today:

"You gotta find what it means to be a soldier. Beat back those that are trying to kill everything that's good and right and call it 'making it great again.' We can't just be citizens in a time of war, that would be surrender. That'd be giving up our future, and our souls. Ain't nobody gets to sit this one out, you hear me?"

ABOUT THE AUTHOR

Lynne Sullivan, MFT, is a licensed Marriage and Family Counselor who graduated cum laude at California State University, Northridge, and holds a Master's degree in Marriage and Family Therapy from the California Family Study Center, aka Campbellsville University

Before pursuing a career as a therapist, Lynne was a writer, actor, and director, and still continues her creative endeavors by writing poetry in her original style. She has a unique way of weaving her expressive arts background into her therapy sessions.

As a professional therapist, Lynne has been a strong advocate of women's rights and has specialized in helping adolescents and young women who are struggling to launch themselves into a stable, productive lifestyle. She has taught parenting for residential treatment workers, focusing on education without shame.

Lynne has also provided tools for traumatized women on how to cope with their Post-Traumatic Stress Disorder to reduce their recidivism while coping with substance abuse, not only in private therapy sessions, but for the county jail system as well.

Lynne has worked in court ordered domestic violence programs to educate men on the misuse of power in their attempts to achieve control. Her keen awareness of justice and equality issues for children, adolescents, and adults has provided her with a much needed perspective on today's struggle for women seeking empowerment.

Lynne often incorporates Mindfulness Meditation skills to assist her clients to enhance their capacity for self-compassion and awareness.

ABOUT THE ILLUSTRATOR

Jorie Martin has created art throughout her lifetime. She earned a Bachelor of Fine Arts degree from Eastern Michigan University and is an alumna of the School of the Art Institute of Chicago. Jorie is an award-winning fine art painter, illustrator, and author who has written and illustrated dozens of books for children and adults.

Being a member of the "transitional generation" of the feminist movement, Jorie endured huge gender inequalities as a young woman, but has seen new laws and attitudes improve life for American women today.

Jorie lives in California with her artist husband, creative children, and amusing pets.

"If they don't give you a seat at the table, bring a folding chair."

– Shirley Chisholm

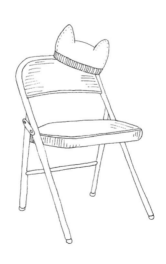

Printed in Great Britain
by Amazon